D1052904

We Need Child Care Workers

by Lisa Trumbauer

Consulting Editor: Gail Saunders-Smith, Ph.D.

Consultant: Sherry Workman, Executive Director, National Association of Child Care Professionals

Pebble Books

an imprint of Capstone Press
Mankato, Minnesota

Pebble Books are published by Capstone Press
151 Good Counsel Drive, P.O. Box 669, Mankato, Minnesota 56002
www.capstonepress.com

062011 006208R

Library of Congress Cataloging-in-Publication Data
Trumbauer, Lisa, 1963–
　　We need child care workers / by Lisa Trumbauer.
　　p. cm.—(Helpers in our community)
　　Summary: Simple text and photographs present child care workers and their
role in the community.
　　Includes bibliographical references and index.
　　ISBN-13: 978-0-7368-1648-9 (hardcover)
　　ISBN-10: 0-7368-1648-8 (hardcover)
　　1. Child care—Juvenile literature.　2. Child care workers—Juvenile literature.
[1. Child care.　2. Child care workers.　3. Occupations.]　I. Title.　II. Series.
HQ778.5.T78　2003
362.71'2—dc21
　　　　　　　　　　　　　　　　　　　　　　　　　　　　　　　2002007678

Note to Parents and Teachers

The Helpers in Our Community series supports national social
studies standards for units related to community helpers and their
roles. This book describes and illustrates child care workers and
how they care for children. The photographs support early readers
in understanding the text. This book also introduces early readers to
subject-specific vocabulary words, which are defined in the Words
to Know section. Early readers may need assistance to read some
words and to use the Table of Contents, Words to Know, Read
More, Internet Sites, and Index/Word List sections of the book.

Table of Contents

Child care workers
take care of children.

Child care workers
keep children safe.

Child care workers
help children learn.

10

Child care workers
read books to children.

Child care workers
help children stay healthy.

14

Child care workers
make snacks.

Child care workers help
children paint pictures.

Child care workers
help children play.

Child care workers
and children have fun.

Words to Know

child care worker—a person who takes care of children when their parents are away

healthy—fit and well

parent—a mother or a father

safe—not in danger of being harmed; child care workers carefully watch children so that they are safe.

snack—a small meal; people often eat snacks between regular meals.

Read More

Ecker, Debbie. *People Work.* Mankato, Minn.: Yellow Umbrella Books, 2000.

Gibson, Karen Bush. *Child Care Workers.* Community Helpers. Mankato, Minn.: Bridgestone Books, 2001.

Senisi, Ellen B. *Hurray for Pre-K!* New York: HarperCollins Publishers, 2000.

Internet Sites

Track down many sites about child care. Visit the FACT HOUND at *http://www.facthound.com*

IT IS EASY! IT IS FUN!

1) Go to *http://www.facthound.com*

2) Type in: 0736816488

3) Click on "FETCH IT" and FACT HOUND will find several links hand-picked by our editors.

Relax and let our pal FACT HOUND do the research for you!

Index/Word List

books, 11
care, 5
fun, 21
healthy, 13
help, 9, 13, 17, 19
keep, 7
learn, 9
make, 15

paint, 17
pictures, 17
play, 19
read, 11
safe, 7
snacks, 15
stay, 13
take, 5

Word Count: 58
Early-Intervention Level: 8

Credits
Mari C. Schuh, editor; Abby Bradford, Bradfordesign, Inc., series designer;
Molly Nei, book designer; Nancy White, photo stylist

Capstone Press/Gary Sundermeyer, cover, 1, 4, 6, 8, 12, 14, 16, 18, 20
Index Stock Imagery/Myrleen Cate, 10

Pebble Books thanks Golden Heart Child Care Center of North Mankato, Minnesota,
and its employees for their helpful assistance with this book.